THE
Irresistible
Church SERIES

D1211327

West Philadelphia
Mennonite Fellowship
4740 Baltimore Avenue
Philadelphia, PA 19143

We've GOT THIS!

We've GOT THIS!

Providing Respite for Families
AFFECTED BY DISABILITY

by Debbie Lillo

 THE IRRESISTIBLE CHURCH SERIES

CONTENTS

Why Respite? 9

Start Digging Your Well 19

Planning for Respite Volunteers 33

Volunteer Training 39

Day of the Event 59

Fresh Water 71

The *Irresistible* Church 73

Why Respite?

Offering respite to parents of a child or teen with disabilities is like digging a freshwater well.

magine being a missionary, called to an underdeveloped country to share the love of Jesus. Families and children in that country are dying of water borne illnesses. Mission groups have tried to serve this region in the past but have lacked cultural sensitivity. Where do you start? How do you begin to rebuild trust? Before you ever begin to talk about Jesus, you might consider building the people a freshwater well. As you provide for their very basic needs, they cannot help but be softened by your compassionate heart. If you earn their trust, then they may be ready to hear about this Savior of yours who guides your every step.

In the same way, providing respite to parents or caretakers of a child or teen with disability offers a cup of cold water from a freshwater well to families who are so very weary and thirsty.

Parents who have one or more children with disabilities are often grieving, overwhelmed, isolated, and exhausted. If they knew God before disability touched their family, chances are high that they have faced a crisis of faith as they encountered disability. If they did not know God, they may not be interested in knowing a God who would allow the challenges they face. Many have had difficult experiences with churches already. Some have been asked to leave. Before we can begin to talk about Jesus, respite allows us to meet a desperate need. In meeting that need, the church opens a door to skeptical parents. This is the beginning of a church moving towards *irresistible*. Once the church has earned their trust, these families will begin to ask, "What is it that motivates you to show such compassion?"

The beauty of respite is that it serves basic needs in an easy-to-plan, low-budget fashion. Respite not only blesses tired and overwhelmed parents, it also is important for the children who have disabilities, their siblings, the volunteers who come to serve, and the church as a whole. *Respite* literally means "a period of rest or relief." Respite events provide parents or caregivers a temporary relief from the responsibilities of caring for individuals with physical or intellectual disabilities. Respite is the gift of time. It is a church outreach activity that draws otherwise cautious families over the threshold and into the church because it meets a valuable and practical need.

Parents Need Respite

Whenever a family first faces disability, a dream has been altered. The loss of that dream or expectation leads to grief—grief that is every bit as real and challenging as the physical death of a loved one.⧳ As parents are grieving, they are simultaneously thrown into a world of intense discovery, uncertainty, added expense, long hours, and emotional exhaustion. Many find that it is no longer easy to be included in social and recreational activities and become increasingly isolated. Marriages grow fragile under the strain of new financial obligations, exhaustion, and the lack of time or energy to work on the marriage relationship. Many parents have—unfortunately—been turned away from churches that were not prepared to include the unique challenges that come with disabilities. Even those who have not yet tried to go to church fear that they might not be accepted, and think inherently that if the church rejects you, it is like having God reject you. Respite events reach out to these families to say, "Jesus cares. The church cares. We have a place for you. We believe your child or loved one has great value in the kingdom of God."

⧳ This symbol indicates that there are supplemental resources that correspond with this topic at http://www.joniandfriends.org/church-relations/

Children and Teens with Disabilities Need Respite

It is important for children with disabilities to know that the church cares. We find that children in special needs ministries love coming to church because they recognize that the people who serve them also love them. By loving these children, we show them that God loves them, which can open the door to teaching them about God's saving grace.

Many community services and events exclude these children, but churches can welcome them to respite events designed especially for them. We can train buddies to help them enjoy the activities provided. Children with disabilities can make new friends of all ages—adults, teens and peers. Often these relationships begin at respite events and continue to grow afterward.

Siblings Need Respite

Brothers and sisters of children and teens with disabilities have unique family lives and challenges. They are generally asked to grow up faster than other kids. Their needs are often considered secondary. Creating an event that includes and focuses on siblings gives them a break from caregiving responsibilities. It helps them see that the church believes they are valuable and important too. It allows them to experience Christ's love through the care they receive from their volunteer buddies.

One of the things siblings often say when we ask why they enjoy respite events is that they get to hang out with other siblings. They discover that there are other kids experiencing similar challenges. As they take time to play together at respite events they grow in confidence and come to see that they are given unique opportunities because of being a special needs family.

"My brother might be a little different," said a 7-year-old sibling after a respite event, "but because of him I get to go to all of these cool church parties and have met lots of fun kids who are just like me!"

As multiple churches in a community embrace respite, these siblings have more and more opportunities to spend time together. As friendships grow, so do the opportunities for community churches to work together to provide intentional sibling support outside of respite. Siblings need to know that the church values them. Each sibling needs to come to understand that God created them with value and purpose and is developing something unique and special in and through their sibling experience.

Respite Volunteers Need Respite

Respite events typically provide three- to four-hour opportunities for church members to step out of their comfort zones and be loved by a child or teen who either has a disability or is a sibling of a child with disabilities. Many first-time volunteers admit to being afraid before a respite event begins, but can be found a short time later smiling and engaged—completely taken in by how little it requires to help these friends feel loved and welcomed. In our experience, over 90% of first-time respite volunteers say they will return. Many go on to be buddies on Sunday mornings. Respite transforms the hearts of timid volunteers!

We cannot emphasize enough how wonderful respite is as a way for youth groups to serve together. When youth leaders communicate the value of service and model compassion for their students, youth rise to the occasion and serve at respite events with excellence. When planning your respite event schedule, be sure to consider a time that is convenient for the youth in your church and include the youth leadership in your vision casting.

Your Church Needs Respite

As your church becomes an intentionally welcoming place for families impacted by disability, more and more church family members will have the opportunity to interact with and be transformed by them. When church leadership sees respite events as church-wide events and encourages a broad section of the church to serve, the church is transformed. Respite volunteers are more likely to intentionally welcome special needs families to church and encourage their peers to do the same.

Suzie[1] is a beautiful 16-year-old who has cerebral palsy. After attending a church's respite events for more than five years, her family decided to begin attending the church on Sunday mornings. Suzie has limited language and poor social awareness, but she loves people. When she rolls into the sanctuary or youth group, it is usually with gleeful—and not always quiet—greetings to those she recognizes. She reaches out to say hello to people she has never met. Many congregations would find Suzie distracting, but this church is filled with respite volunteers who have come to appreciate her. They know that she loves Jesus and they smile when she shouts "Amen" at the end of prayers. They have learned to help her focus on the pastor's face when he speaks. She has helped her church to care less about "tidiness" and more about compassion.

The Body of Christ Needs Respite

One of the greatest blessings that comes from the respite movement is seeing how it brings churches

Note
1. Not real name

together. One church in a community can only effectively offer a limited number of respite events each year. Two churches double that number. Three to four churches working together allow families to experience respite many times each year. In order for this to happen, schedules and vision need to be shared. Eventually, volunteers and supplies might be shared. Suddenly these families that many see as "broken" have built bridges between churches previously unengaged with one another. The Body of Christ is unified, and our Father must indeed be pleased!

The Gospel Is Advanced Through Respite

When a church family offers respite events, it acts as Jesus' hands and feet. Volunteers offer that cup of fresh water to families who are so very dry and depleted.

Most respite events are not specifically evangelistic in nature, but the church does earn the trust and confidence of families by meeting a basic and urgent need. As these families see that respite volunteers truly value them, hearts are softened to hear the message of the gospel. They begin to believe that God desires them to be part of the church body. By reaching out to meet practical needs, the church shows families affected by disability the hope of Christ and the love of the Father.

Without a biblical perspective, parents can feel their children were born by mistake or because of an uncaring God. They can become overwhelmed because they see little productive purpose in their family's experiences. When churches reach out to serve these families, their hearts can be softened to the Word of God. Respite events demonstrate the congregation's belief in the value of their children and in the truth that the Lord knit each child together in his or her mother's womb and that each one is fearfully and wonderfully made (Psalm 139:13-16). The little children are welcomed in Jesus' name (Matthew 18:5) and the work of God is displayed in their lives (John 9:1-3). Scripture comes alive as evidence that their children are purposefully and lovingly created by God, and he desires for them to know him and have fellowship with his people.

In summary, respite events provide a wonderful way for families to cross the threshold of the church with very little risk. Otherwise cautious families are often willing to attend events because their need for respite is great. The people of the church are able to put their faith into action by loving families in very practical ways. As families receive that love, they become more open to hearing the saving message of the gospel.

"Asking me how I will spend my respite time is like handing me a million dollars and telling me I need to decide right now how to spend it."

MOTHER OF AN 8-YEAR-OLD BOY WITH AUTISM

"They were so kind and accepting. It makes me want to come back."

MOTHER WITH A SPECIAL NEEDS CHILD
FROM OUTSIDE THE CHURCH

"We haven't had a date for 8 years since she was born. Thank you!"

MOTHER OF A CHILD WITH CEREBRAL PALSY
AND GLOBAL DELAYS

Start Digging Your Well

Step 1:
Commit to Ongoing Prayer

Respite is only an effective outreach tool if it is Spirit directed and within God's will for your church. Before taking any steps towards this decision, bathe it in prayer. Gather a team who is committed to praying for every aspect of your planning and implementation. Seek God's guidance and celebrate his victories. Continue to pray at every stage of your first respite event and those to come.

Step 2:
Consider if Your Church Is Prepared to Welcome Respite Families on Sunday Mornings

When engaging in respite ministry churches should consider how they can include these families in the everyday life of the church. Teachers in the children and youth departments can be trained so they are prepared to welcome respite families who want to take the next steps toward getting involved. Church staff and lay leaders should understand and be prepared to answer difficult questions families might have about God and why he allowed their family to be affected by disabilities.

Welcoming a family to respite and then saying, "Sorry, we do not have a plan to include your child in the life of our church" gives a mixed message. We want to invite these families to the foot of the cross. We need to think through how we can welcome these families into the body of Christ long-term before we begin outreach.

You can reference Joni and Friends' book *Start With Hello* to learn more about starting a disability ministry at your church. It can also be helpful to connect with your local Joni and Friends office. They can help point you to the most current resources to prepare your church for these children and youth.

Step 3:
Decide the Best Day of the Week, Time, and Event Style

Respite programs are typically offered on Friday nights, Saturday mornings, Saturday afternoons, and Saturday nights. While most respite events take place at a church, they can also be held at any central location in the community like a park, community center or YMCA. Some churches host monthly, less structured programs that have a small group of volunteers watching the children "in a group." These events need fewer volunteers and can allow families more frequent opportunities for a cup of fresh water in the form of respite. The most common model is to plan a larger event that encourages more members of the church to participate. These are often scheduled quarterly or during holiday seasons. While planning your respite event, take time to consider the schedule of your church, your potential volunteers and what would most interest individuals within your community. For your first respite event, we encourage you to choose a three- to four-hour time frame that works best for your church and the potential volunteers.

Note: *You should also consider the respite schedules of other churches in your area that already host respite events. It is wonderful when churches across the community coordinate care so that families can receive respite more frequently than one church alone could provide.*

Step 4:
Decide the Target Age of the Participants

Next decide the age group you will target. The events described in this book are structured as children's programs, but they can easily be modified if you plan to include high-functioning teens and adults, or if you include youth siblings. Many respite events limit the developmental age to 12. Many teens and young adults with cognitive delays have enjoyed respite events if they do not mind doing kids' activities and if their buddies treat them as teens and young adults, not kids. It can be difficult to have a sibling older than 12 unless you know them well, have an intentional teen sibling program planned, and/or can use them as helpers. Some teen siblings feel they have been dragged to "baby" activities, and if so, it will not be a supportive or productive environment for them.

Step 5:

Determine Space and Rooms Available for Respite Events

Preschool classrooms make wonderful respite rooms as they are already equipped for children and are not filled with things that could easily be damaged. Nurseries are good for younger children and sometimes for older children with cognitive delays who like the typical cause-and-effect toys. If your church has a playground or secure outside area, children enjoy outdoor play. It is also nice to have a larger room to hold recreation and special events if possible. Youth rooms are wonderful for older siblings. If you are using rooms that are set up for school or Sunday use, ask teachers to put valuable or sentimental things away. Always be mindful to leave the rooms as you found them. Kids who attend respite events are not more destructive than typical kids, but this allows your leadership to focus on the children and volunteers.

Step 6:
Consider Your Potential Volunteer Pool

You will want to consider who is likely to volunteer for a respite event. Look for youth leaders who are trying to engage students in service. If you use youth ministry students, it can be helpful for their leaders to be there too, helping them to stay more focused on service than socializing. Are there empty nesters in the congregation who would love to play with children? Are there members who are trained in special education or who seem particularly drawn to kids with special needs? Do your adult small groups tend to serve together? You may find that respite events will attract a whole new group of volunteers. No expertise is required in order to do an excellent job. Churches can typically use their regular children's ministry volunteer applications and background check policies.

Step 7:
Determine Potential Event Activities

We will discuss actual scheduling in the "Day of the Event" section. However, your initial planning should include some basic decisions about what sorts of activities you want to include. Have fun with this process! Consider the talents of your leadership team and resources available to you as you determine what to include. The events you choose will determine many of the leadership and volunteer decisions to follow. Respite events often include:

Crafts: Most kids with special needs enjoy simple crafts, but may need help from their buddies due to their limited dexterity. Simple crafts can be created using basic items such as paper, tempera paint, stamps, foam stickers or large paint tubes designed for kids who cannot grasp a brush. Add more craft steps to projects for kids who are higher functioning and for siblings. Many congregations have someone who is gifted in creating simple crafts and could provide a variety of craft options. To add greater interest tie craft time to a special theme such as Advent, Christmas or Valentine's Day and make gifts for parents, caretakers and friends.

Music: If you have someone who plays the guitar and loves to lead singing, this is a wonderful opportunity for them to serve! You could also have an engaging time of music using a CD player, fun kids' handheld musical instruments, and some ribbon wands. By and large, kids with disabilities LOVE music and are easily engaged by rhythm and movement. For a few children, it may be too noisy and chaotic. Those kids may return to their individual recreational activities or take a walk with their buddy. They might be able to participate wearing a sound-filtering headset or watching from a distance. Again, our goal is to help the kids have fun—not to force them to do activities they do not enjoy.

Group Recreation: Most children enjoy being part of a group recreation period. If you choose to have the kids play in a sandbox, consider leading into the activity with a parade around the sandbox. Children usually enjoy games and activities with a large rainbow parachute and are fascinated by fun things to hurl into the air.

Individual Recreation: Some children, especially those on the autism spectrum, may not want to participate in group recreational activities. That is fine—this is supposed to be fun! For these kids, offer a variety of individual activities such as therapy balls, a wading pool filled with plastic balls or scooter boards that can be pulled with rope. They may also like to chase bubbles or simply escape to a quiet tent.

Snack Time: Depending on what time your respite event will take place, you may want to consider serving a light meal or snack. Ensure that children with food allergies receive snacks brought by their families. Be watchful to see that children eat their own snacks and not their neighbors'. Food allergies should be noted on each child's registration form. Many respite events make it a practice to only serve gluten-free, nut-free, dairy-free snacks. This allows most kids with food allergies to eat what everyone else is eating.

Wind-Down Activities: Consider gathering the children for a quiet story or video at the end of the event to ensure that the children are calm when their parents return. This is a good opportunity to share a Bible story or show a Bible-focused video such as VeggieTales.

Community Participation and Special Events: A wonderful way to engage the broader community in your respite event is to start a presentation rotation schedule. Community service providers often have short programs they have prepared for children. Check with local firefighters, police departments, youth science institutes, petting zoos, companion dog trainers, etc. Individuals may also be interested in bringing animals for a petting zoo or guide dogs in training.

Children's clubs and organizations in your area may help you locate magicians, jugglers, puppeteers, choirs or other entertainers that they can recommend. Children enjoy these special programs and may want to invite their friends.

In addition to providing enjoyable programs for kids, this is another wonderful opportunity to show your community that your congregation values these families enough to offer this kind of care.

Theme: Many churches hosting respite events have found that it is fun to add a theme to each event and plan the craft and recreation activities around that theme. Themes could include farm day, circus day, upcoming holidays, cowboys, and zoo day. Often themes can be tied to community events or to VBS curriculum so that craft ideas and decorations can be recycled.

Step 8:
Begin Recruiting Your Leadership Team

Look for leaders with organizational skills, music skills, recreational skills, and nursing experience who might volunteer their time. There is a list of leadership roles in the next section, *"Planning for Respite Volunteers."*

Step 9:
Begin to Gather Respite Tools

There are probably many materials already available at your church that can be used for respite events. Joni and Friends offers a "Respite Resources List"📚 that our event leaders have found helpful to have on hand. If your church has preschool, children's, or youth classrooms check there before purchasing items.

Simple backpacks or drawstring bags can be purchased at dollar stores and used as "buddy bags" to carry items that help your buddy navigate his/her universe. These bags can be personalized once you have received registration forms on each child. Items you may want to include are:

- Schedule for the day
- Map of church campus with rooms labeled for how they will be used the day of your event

- Communication Board with crayon
- Page of emotion faces and/or icons to help non-verbal children communicate through pictures
- Timer (dollar store variety)
- Sensory toys
- Identification badge (with or without photo)

A more detailed list of buddy bag items and examples can be found in the online resources accompanying this book.

Step 10:
Decide if You Will Offer a Kick-Off Training Event

Many successful respite events include 45 minutes of pre-event training. Extra training and awareness is always a plus. However, sometimes volunteers are willing to serve but are not willing to give up an additional afternoon or evening for pre-training. You will know what training format will best fit your congregation. A training prior to the church's first respite event is a wonderful way to spread the vision and calm fears of potential first-time volunteers. You will find tools for planning a training session in the "Volunteer Training" section.

Step 11:
Decide How Many Children You Hope to Serve

After determining potential volunteers, you are ready to decide how many children the respite program can serve. A good rule of thumb is to try and have one volunteer for each child with a disability and one volunteer for every one to two siblings, plus a leadership team.

Step 12:
Decide Who Will Handle Registration and How Families Will Register

We have found that it is easy for parents to RSVP by email and be emailed a registration form in return. This will allow you to keep all of the communication in a single folder. You should identify who will receive and manage the registrations and how parents can return the registration forms (email, postal mail, in person, etc.). It can be a good idea to hold face-to-face interviews with new parents to better understand the child's care needs. In the online resources corresponding with this book, Joni and Friends offers a sample respite application that can be personalized to your church's needs.

Step 13:

Determine How You Will Advertise

Included in the online supplemental materials for this book, you will find a sample of a respite flyer.≋ Once you create a flyer for your event, consider how it can be used to get the word out. If there are already churches in your area doing respite, will their families be invited? Are there special needs families already attending your church who might also want to invite friends? Do you know school teachers who could invite their students? Do you have access to regional center case workers who know which families would benefit most? The first event is typically the hardest because parents do not yet know your church. There is no track record of successful respite events, and you do not necessarily know the families in the community who would benefit. Encourage your team to pray for God's leading. He knows the right families to be reached, and they can invite their friends. Remember that this event can be an amazing outreach opportunity!

Step 14:

Investigate Your Church's Liability Policies

We encourage churches to check with their insurance companies and any other church agents who deal with liability issues pertaining to events. Many respite events choose to have a volunteer nurse on site during the event as it can help parents feel more comfortable. If you choose to have nurses at your event, you will need to determine if they are required to carry their own liability insurance. Churches do not generally need to take out an additional policy or add liability—insurance companies usually treat respite events as they would VBS or other drop-off programs. But we encourage you to check as each community's issues are unique.

Step 15:
Review Your Church's Health and Emergency Procedures

Review the church's normal emergency procedures with all the volunteers at training times and before the start of the event. Volunteers need to know who to contact and how to contact them in case of an emergency, as well as all evacuation and take-cover plans. You will find more details about specific health and safety concerns in the "Day of Event" section.

Planning for Respite Volunteers

Once you have taken the first steps towards planning a respite event, you are ready to concentrate on one of the most important aspects of planning—recruiting volunteers. This section will discuss two types of critical volunteers: volunteers with specific role assignments and respite buddies.

Volunteers with Specific Roles

Respite events tend to be more successful when you consider the role of each volunteer and pray about the right person for each role. Every church's respite event will be unique, but your leadership team might include:

1. A **Program Coordinator** organizes the registration and advertisement for the event including creation of flyers and handouts, as well as bulletins and local press releases.

2. A **Volunteer Coordinator** finds and schedules volunteers, keeps track of volunteers as they arrive and makes last-minute buddy decisions if volunteers or families do not come.

3. A **Crafts Coordinator** plans the crafts, collects or purchases the materials for the crafts, and trains the other crafts volunteers to supervise at craft stations.

4. A **Music Leader** plans and leads music.

5. A **Snack Leader** plans the food for training, oversees the children's snacks, as well as optional treats for the volunteers when they take breaks.

6. A **Training Leader** plans the day-of-event training and communicates with the registration leader so that volunteers are trained to care for the children who have registered.

7. A **Volunteer Nurse** meets with parents during check-in to ensure that pertinent information and day-of-event contact information is included on their children's registration forms.

During the event, the nurse helps with minor injuries and sees that children with allergies are given the correct foods. The nurse determines if parents and/or EMTs need to be contacted in cases of seizures, illnesses or major injuries. This person (with another adult present) may also change diapers for older children who need such assistance.

8. A **Buddy Bag/Sensory Toy Collector** gathers materials and equipment to create buddy bags and provide appropriate sensory materials for the children attending.

9. An **Optional Leader for each age group** rotates with the group during the events and helps with any issues that arise. This role is particularly helpful if your respite event will keep all age groups together during rotations.

10. **Floaters and Door Attendants**: It is nice to have at least one "floater" who can fill in wherever needed and provide bathroom breaks and snack breaks for the volunteers. Also, consider the building layout and the number of entrances and exits. You may

want to have a person assigned to prevent unauthorized entrances or exits (especially if you have a child who is a known "runner" in the group).

The above positions are not exhaustive by any means and can be combined, split, and changed to meet the needs of your specific event and the volunteers you have available.

Respite Buddies

Respite buddies will work one-on-one with children who have disabilities and/or the siblings. Note that younger siblings can be paired with other siblings their same sex and general age, but the more personal attention they get the more they will feel like the event has been planned especially for them. Older siblings may particularly enjoy spending their time with their leaders rather than in the large group setting. Those siblings may not ever join in on the group activities designed for the younger children, or they may join for music or special events.

Be creative as you recruit volunteers. Visit other churches' respite events so that you can tell firsthand stories of families and volunteers being blessed by respite. Ask if you might take some pictures so that your flyers and advertisement can include compelling images. Contact your local Joni and Friends office for suggestions on inspirational videos and other materials that might help soften your congregation's heart for your upcoming event. Whether it is from the pulpit or in a smaller meeting, cast vision for ongoing respite support. The supplemental online resources for this book include customizable forms and examples related to volunteers, including applications, sign-up sheets and FAQ sheets.

Volunteer Training

Training for Your First Event

Many churches have held successful respite events by holding day-of-event-training. Others choose to offer a special training a month or so ahead of the respite event to allow for more in-depth disability awareness training and to get volunteers excited about the upcoming event.

The advantage of more in-depth training is that your volunteers will be better prepared and will need less guidance during the event itself. It can also serve as a volunteer recruitment opportunity for the event if part of the training is spent discussing why families need respite. The disadvantage is that it adds one or two hours to the volunteers' commitments, and you may lose some potential volunteers whose schedules are already full.

Later in this section we offer a sampling of training activities that can help potential volunteers better understand what it is like to walk in the shoes of the families and children they will support at respite events. These activities will also give them tools for interacting with their new friends with respect and confidence.

Extended first-time training will allow your volunteers to experience more of these activities and to hear more about why your church feels called to offer respite and overall inclusion to the families you will serve. It will give your volunteers knowledge and skills beyond what they can learn while working with an individual child at respite. It will also give you the opportunity to explain a biblical perspective of disability ministry. For more detailed information on a biblical perspective of disability ministry please visit www.joniandfriends.org/BYS/.

Day-of-Event Training

Day-of-event training is time limited and should be tailored to prepare the volunteers for the children they will serve that day. We hope that the training suggestions we offer here will get you started, but we also encourage you to be creative and offer a fresh take on training each time you offer a respite event. The following items are the core of what you might consider including:

- Prayer
- The biblical perspective on embracing families affected by disability
- Disability sensitivity training with a focus on the disabilities that will be represented at the event

- A clear description of volunteer roles
- A confidentiality reminder
- Your expectations and rules for the day
- A review of safety procedures

As mentioned earlier, it is beneficial to be sure that volunteer applications and screenings conform to your church's guidelines. This is particularly important if you have invited volunteers from outside of your congregation to participate.

A Typical Day-of-Event Respite Training Outline

1. Open in prayer.
2. Make sure that everyone has a disability etiquette handout. ☙ Explain that it is a great tool and that you will only cover the parts of it that are relevant to the kids who are coming that day, but these are things to be mindful of in everyday life.
3. Read Psalm 139 located at the top of the sheet. Encourage volunteers to look up other verses later. God fully values all of his creations and wants us to draw them into his church. Respite will often draw otherwise cautious families into the church because the events meet their needs.

4. Reiterate how most of the parents who participate are exhausted and isolated. They are often "on" most waking hours of the day, and have very little opportunity to rest and reflect. Couples rarely have time to talk. Respite events give them a HUGE gift. Encourage volunteers to share how they spend their leisure time and reflect on what it would feel like to not have any downtime.

5. Work through the sensitivity sheet quickly, highlighting the disabilities that will be represented.

6. Pass a clipboard that posts the statement "I promise to keep all information about my buddy confidential." Have each volunteer sign the sheet.

7. Go through the day's schedule, the volunteer roles, safety policies, and the check-in process.

8. Remind volunteers that all information about the families is confidential and should not be shared with others—even with their friends in the room. All intake forms should be collected before volunteers leave the room.

9. Allow time for questions and answers. Remind volunteers that one of our key phrases for parents is "We've Got This!"

10. Pray

11. Have fun!!!

Training Tools

Disability Etiquette: Responding with Compassion

You will find a printable version ☙ of Joni and Friends' Disability Etiquette handout in the online supplemental resources webpage. Have handouts ready for each volunteer at your training. This document will give you "talking points" as you prepare your volunteers to work with the children who are coming to your event.

All Individuals Are Purposefully and Lovingly Created by God

For you created my inmost being; you knit me together in my mother's womb. I praise you because I am fearfully and wonderfully made; your works are wonderful, I know that full well.—Psalm 139:13-16 NIV

Other verses to ponder: John 9:1-3, Matthew 9:36-37, 2 Corinthians 1:3-4, Luke 14: 21-23

Training Illustration: The Weight of Raising a Child with Disabilities

Materials needed: 5-10 large building blocks

Ask for a volunteer to come to the front of the room and stand next to you and use the below script to visually display the strain that parents and caretakers experience.

> *Through our respite event we are giving some exhausted parents a rest. I would like to use some blocks to help you get a sense of the fatigue most of these parents experience.*
>
> *Many of these children live with serious health issues. For example, one child coming to our respite event (use a real story if you are able to) had five or six surgeries in her first year of life. Many have immune deficiencies and frequently visit doctors or hospitals. This block represents all the medical decisions and stressors families with children affected by disability must carry.*
>
> *(Hand one block to the volunteer, adding more blocks to his or her arms with each pressure you describe.)*
>
> *When a family learns that their child has or will have a disability, they begin to research the specific diagnosis. They become advocates for that child and must make many decisions about giving their son or daughter the best care possible. This block represents all of the advocacy decisions these parents must make on an ongoing basis.*
>
> *Most of these kids receive several types of therapy, frequently resulting in multiple appointments every week. Parents must schedule, coordinate, and even*

participate with therapies. They may assist speech therapists, occupational therapists, physical therapists, behavior therapists, educational therapists... it is a daunting list. This block represents all of the therapies families must coordinate.

Often there are other children in the family, and parents must figure out how to give them adequate attention and support. Understandably, some siblings go through difficult stages and can resent the attention their parents must give a child with special needs. This block is for the stress of parenting siblings.

These parents expected to have typically developing children. Even if they adore their son or daughter with disabilities, many hopes and dreams for that child have been altered. When expectations do not come to pass, true grief follows. This block is for the continual grief process, and for the toll it takes on the parents' emotional stability.

Not surprisingly, there are stressful divorces among some couples dealing with grief, painful decisions, and little time to work on their marriage. This block is for the stressful marriages.

We could keep going with things such as endless reports, meetings with school officials, the difficulties of simply getting out of the door or being in public, but you get the point!

(Turn to the volunteer who is now buried in blocks.)

Are the blocks heavy? Go ahead and put them down.

(The helper will probably be unable to put the blocks down without assistance.)

The same is true for the parents: They are exhausted. They are stressed. They are buried in the unique demands of their lives. They need churches to walk alongside and care for them—to show them the love of Christ in supportive, practical ways.

This is a good opportunity to define the difference between pity and compassion:

Pity: *I am standing without any blocks in my hands, looking at you with all your blocks and feeling sorry for you. Almost always, I am looking down on you. And I am making myself feel better by doing something for you.*

Compassion: *I see that a brother or sister is carrying a heavy load. I look them in the eye—as an equal—and offer to walk alongside and lighten the load.*

Sample Disability Simulation Activities

Role-Playing

Allow the volunteers you are training to experience life through the eyes of disability. This exercise can take place during a meal or any other activity that takes place in a different room, ideally down some stairs or away from the training classroom.

Materials needed: Secure several manual wheelchairs, duct tape, bandanas, sunglasses, Vaseline, communication board and earplugs.

1. Ask everyone to choose a partner, and then give each pair one of the following scenarios:

   a. You do not have use of your legs, use of your arms is limited, and you must use a wheelchair. Use an ace bandage or duct tape to limit mobility.

   b. You have limited dexterity with your fingers. Use duct tape to attach several of your fingers together on both hands.

   c. You have no vision. Please have your partner tie a bandana over your eyes and guide you.

    d. You have limited vision. Please wear sunglasses coated with Vaseline. You will be asked to read aloud to the group during the meal.

    e. You have an auditory deficit. Please put earplugs firmly in both ears.

    f. You cannot talk. Please use the communication board provided whenever you need to speak.

2. Ask one member of each pair to pretend to have the described disability. His/her partner should act as the assistant.

3. Halfway through the activity each pair should make their way back to the meeting room in his/her first role and then switch roles.

Disability Simulation Stations

If "experiencing" a disability by journeying outside your training room for a meal or other activity is not an option, an alternate training scenario can be done by breaking the participants into small groups and rotating those groups through the below stations. Because they will not be experiencing this role-playing over a meal or some longer activity, this scenario can require more facilitators to ensure that participants understand the activities and to encourage discussion about the experiences. Here are some good activities to choose, depending on your space, time and facilitators.

1. Wheelchair Experiences

Supplies needed: wheelchairs, barriers, and objects to carry

Instructions: Ask partners to switch midway through the activity. Practice carrying-on a conversation with your partner in a wheelchair. Notice how his/her neck could become stiff if you stand in front. Each partner should practice navigating an obstacle course with a manual chair. Their partner should watch for obstacles and assist if requested. Each partner should try to overcome a difficult obstacle without help.

2. Sensory Overload

Note: This can also be done as a group activity. Have one to three volunteers sit on chairs in the front of the room. Ask them to read the book out loud. One at a time, add a sensory overload activity. As you do, explain how this affects an individual with sensory sensitivities.

Supplies needed: 3 chairs, 3 CD players with headphones, something scratchy to place on each chair, 3 shirts with tags taped inside the collars, 3 feather dusters, something smelly, something for each group to read and answer questions about, and 3 flashlights.

Instructions: Many individuals with autism, ADHD or learning disabilities are particularly sensitive to noise and other sensory bombardments. Ask one partner to wear the shirt with a rough collar, put on the headphones and sit in the "scratchy" chair. While he or she tries to read a passage aloud, the partner brushes around the head and shoulders with a feather duster, flashes the light in the reader's eyes, and puts the smelly item close. Then the partner asks questions like "What are you reading? What does it mean? Do you need any help?" After the passage is over, the reader should answer questions about what was just read. Switch.

3. *Visual Deficits*

Supplies needed: several pairs of sunglasses, Vaseline in small containers, eye masks, and dowel sticks cut to cane-length

Instructions:

Blurred Vision: Using the sunglasses and Vaseline, rub a semi-thick film of Vaseline over the outside lens. When the person put them on, he or she will not be totally blind, but will definitely have a hard time seeing things clearly. The partner will need to assist him or her in any way that might be helpful.

Complete Blindness: Use the eye mask and dowel. Place eye mask completely over one person's eyes so nothing can be seen. Use the dowel as a red-tip cane to assist and alert. The partner who is blind can ask for help with objects that may obstruct the path. The other partner can assist in ways that are helpful for safe movement.

4. *Hearing Loss*

Supplies needed: earplugs, children's storybook

Instructions: Participants work in pairs. One person puts earplugs in his/her ears and listens to the partner read a children's story in a very soft voice. This is most effective if the partner who is reading does not give direct eye contact.

5. *Communication Disorders*

Supplies needed: communication boards, ᘏ straws, and prompts for question-asking

Instructions: One partner is not allowed to speak whatsoever to the other partner or to anyone else in the group. The partner who is nonverbal can use only the alphabet communication board and the straw, as a pointer, to spell out words. Partners should switch halfway through the designated time so that each one can experience being nonverbal.

Example phrases to spell out:

> My name is (include your name).
> Jesus loves you.
> Spell a sentence with at least 5 words.

See if the person across from you can figure out what you are trying to communicate.

6. *Impaired Manual Dexterity*

Supplies needed: Various items of clothing that need buttoning/tying/zipping, gloves or tube socks, duct tape, piggy bank and coins, peanut butter and crackers, and plastic knives

Instructions: Participants work in pairs to accomplish several tasks. For each task, one partner is either wearing gloves that have fingers taped, or has several fingers taped together. Try one or multiple of the following activities: buttoning or zipping clothing; tying shoes; putting pennies in a piggy bank; spreading peanut butter on a cracker and feeding it to your partner. Switch roles so both partners can experience the difficulty of impaired manual dexterity.

7. *Intellectual Disability*

Instructions: One partner represents the person who has an intellectual disability by only using three words or less when communicating with the other partner. If too many questions or too many options are given at one time, look confused and do not answer. Make your partner rethink how to ask the questions in a simpler way.

Debriefing Activities

Whether you have your training participants take part in the first role-playing activity, or experience disability simulations at stations, it is important to allow time to debrief. Usually, discussion can be prompted by asking questions like:

- How did it feel to suddenly have those limitations?
- What was the hardest thing for you?
- Did these activities change the way you will relate to an individual with a disability in the future?

Blessing of the Hands—A Wonderful Send-Off Blessing

As you complete training, you are sending your volunteers out to serve in varying capacities. Some jobs may be challenging, some may feel insignificant. Below is a blessing that has been adapted from a blessing written by Deaconess/Hospital Chaplain Margy Whitsett and the Lutheran Deaconess Association. We have found that this blessing can be used to remind your volunteers how important every job is and to encourage them as they head out to serve.

Bless the hands so big and small
Bless the hands that reach out to all
Bless the hands that give parents a break
Bless the hands that give and don't take

Bless the hands that have no fears
Bless the hands that wipe the tears
Bless the hands that love to teach
Bless the hands that help them reach

Bless the hands that push the chairs
Bless the hands that close in prayers
Bless the hands that lift the cup
Bless the hands that give thumbs up

Bless the hands in song and dance
Bless the hands that change the pants
Bless the hands that play a tune
Bless the hands that lift their spoon

Bless the hands that help the sick
    Bless the hands that have to be quick
Bless the hands that help them swim
    Bless the hands that work in the gym

Bless the hands that love to sign
    Bless the hands that are gentle and kind
Bless the hands that make the plans
    Bless the hands that wash the pans

Bless the hands that lift and clean
    Bless the hands that work with teens
Bless the hands that hold a child
    Bless these hands for a long, long while

Bless the hands that calm the nerves
    Bless the hands that love to serve
Bless the hands that make them laugh
    Bless the hands that belong to staff

Bless the hands that aren't afraid to touch
    Bless the hands that Jesus loves so much
Bless these hands Lord, that are dedicated to you
    Bless these hands that are yours to work through

Bless these hands with power from above
    Bless these hands to deliver your love
As these hands go out and volunteer
    May they always know your presence is near

Day of the Event

Set Up

It is not always possible if the space is being used for something before your event, but some churches find that it is easiest to set up the afternoon before a morning event or the morning/early afternoon before an evening event. If you are setting up just before the event, plan on at least one hour before training to arrange the stations, check the area for items that should be put away, set-up refreshments, and to pray before the volunteers arrive.

Day-of-Event Training

As the previous section explained, it is critical to offer a training event at least an hour before the event begins so that volunteers' hearts will be prepared and they will have the training and sensitivity to love the children and their families well. It should include enough time to explain the schedule, distribute and explain buddy bags if available, share emergency and safety guidelines, and allow volunteers to become familiar with the facilities being used.

The online resources for this book include a sample schedule sheet with volunteer assignments. It is a good idea to have a schedule completed ahead of time in pencil, but expect to make some last-minute buddy switches during training.

Check-In

The nurse should be positioned at the check-in table 15 minutes before parents are due to arrive. After the training is over, it is helpful to have the program coordinator assist with check-in. Here is a list of what you might need at the registration table.

1. **Registration Forms** for all registered children. We encourage you to check with the administration of your church to see if they have a standard media release to incorporate with your registration form. Including a media release will allow you to use photos and videos from your event to advertise for future events.

2. **Name Tags** for all registered children with names written in the same color as their group, if you have the children divided. *Caution: Do not put last names on children's name tags if you plan to take pictures during the event. Identify a specific name tag color for children whose parents or caretakers have not signed a media release.*

3. **Special Instruction Forms** to note any changes since the registration form was completed. ☙

4. **Nurses Form** (1-2 copies) to track medical needs, feeding schedules, etc. It is helpful to have this all in one place. ☙ We encourage you to check with the administration of your church to see if they have standard policies and forms already in place for their children's ministry.

5. **Extra Name Tag Labels** to mark diaper bags, snack bags and other personal items.

6. **Permanent Markers, Pens and Pencils** for labeling.

7. **Digital Thermometer** in case children arrive who appear to be ill.

8. **Hand Sanitizer** for buddies whose children are more susceptible to disease transmission.

9. **Ziploc Bags** for the snacks families bring.

Check-In Rooms and Groups

It helps to divide the children by developmental age groups. This allows activities to be done in smaller groups and can help keep bigger children from stumbling over smaller children. It also provides a place where each child begins the event and helps parents know where to pick their child up at the end of the respite event.

Schedules

In the supplemental online resources you will find several examples of respite event schedules. We have found that it is easiest to create one sheet for each volunteer that shows the schedule and has space to include their specific volunteer assignment. This becomes a great reference tool for the volunteers throughout the event.

Each church is unique and each leadership team has a unique preference for schedule flexibility or rigidity. You may find that your program works best with the children divided into groups that rotate through rooms or stations. You may be holding your event in a large gym that lends itself better to more open movement between activity options. You may find that you have a large group of very small children and several tall, strong children who would potentially endanger the little ones if they were to be playing in the same room. Prayerfully, you will settle into a schedule for your first event based on the children that attend and their unique needs. It is a great idea to have a debrief time before planning your second event.

Many children with disabilities find activities they particularly like and decide to stay there. Encourage your volunteers to allow children to relax and have fun. It is not so important at a respite event to keep a firm schedule or to accomplish set goals. These events are not like school or therapy appointments. The goal is to keep children safe and give parents a break. As a result, schedules become a way to keep order and give volunteers options to do with the children, but they do not need to be rigidly kept.

You can view a sample icon schedule❧ in the online supplemental resources that may help children who particularly like order and routine. It can be used to foreshadow changes by pointing to what is coming next and saying to the child, "In five minutes..." It can also be used to point to what you plan to do, "First we will... Next we will..." Laminated icon buddy boards❧ help children choose activities and keep track of time.

The Role of Respite Lead During an Event

Volunteers will be much more confident if they know that they can ask questions along the way and that someone is available to help with challenges that may arise. The Respite Lead should keep an open eye for potential challenges and be ready with suggestions and encouragements. Remember to complement your volunteers whenever you can and watch for volunteers who seem tired, giving them a break. In the same way, keep an eye out for buddies who are struggling to keep up with their matches, and make assignment switches when needed. This role is to be a shepherd and cheer-leader, and the enthusiasm of the person in this role will set the tone for the day.

Health and Safety Concerns During an Event

Sometimes church leaders and volunteers hesitate to offer respite events because they anticipate health and safety concerns. These fears are usually not an issue, but we recommend having a nurse on hand during your event as a "security blanket" for anxious volunteers and protective parents. As we noted earlier, the nurse typically helps with check-in to ensure that parents have left contact phone numbers, as well as pertinent medical and allergy information. This individual oversees snack collection and distribution and also handles allergy issues. They (along with a second adult) change diapers for children older than those typically needing diaper changes, and they administer first aid to decide if medical needs are serious. Please keep in mind that most children with disabilities are not medically fragile. It is, however, helpful to create clear health and safety policies. These are best communicated clearly in writing to volunteers and parents alike.

Medications

It is good practice to ask parents or caregivers to administer all medication before or after respite events. Non-nurse volunteers and staff leaders should never administer medication. In extreme cases—if and only if the volunteer nurse feels comfortable—arrangements may be made to administer time-sensitive medications such as allergy or asthma medicine. In those cases, clear written instructions and permission slips should be signed and left by the parent. Check with your church's administration to see if they have policies and forms already in place for their children's ministry.

Safety Procedures

Every time a volunteer handles blood, bodily fluids or bodily discharges they should wear latex-free gloves.

Many children are allergic to latex and peanuts, so it can be smart to have respite events totally latex and nut-free.

Volunteers should wash their hands after accompanying a child to the restroom, after assisting a child with wiping his or her nose and before food preparation. Children should wash hands after using the restroom and before eating. During cold and flu season, it is a good idea to provide small hand sanitizer bottles to any buddy working with a child who is prone to illness.

Illnesses

It is generally a good rule of thumb to ask parents to keep children home from respite events if they have any of the following symptoms of illness:

- Fever greater than 99 degrees
- Runny nose with green discharge
- Rashes that have not been identified as allergy-related
- Deep cough
- Diarrhea
- Active chicken pox
- Measles
- Mumps

- Conjunctivitis (Pink Eye)
- Lice
- Ringworm

Although it is difficult to turn families away, sick children should not be admitted to the respite event. We suggest that a digital thermometer with disposable sleeves be available for the nurse to use at check-in. If a child develops symptoms during the event, the nurse should be notified and the parents called to pick up the child. If the child is being treated for an infection with antibiotics he/she must be on the prescribed medication for at least 24 hours prior to the event.

Toileting

If a child needs assistance in the bathroom, follow your normal church procedure. At a minimum, there should never be one adult alone in the bathroom with a child. If a child can use the toilet independently, the buddy should wait outside the door.

Many respite event teams choose to have their volunteer nurse be responsible for toileting children who are older than 2 years of age requiring help in this area. No volunteer, including the nurse, should change a child's diaper without another adult present.

Never Alone in a Room

Volunteers should always avoid being alone with one child in a room, unless the entire room is clearly visible to someone watching in the hallway.

Incident Reports

If a serious issue occurs during the respite event, i.e. an injury, playground equipment breaks, abusive behavior, etc., you should use your church's regular incident reporting forms. Parents should always be notified if their child was involved in a serious incident or hurt in any way during the event.

Confidentiality

All information on a child's registration form is confidential and should only be seen by event leadership, the nurse, and the assigned buddy. Great care should be taken to keep any copies of the forms in the training room and to avoid leaving forms out during or after the event.

As Your Event Comes to an End

You may want to consider offering movie time or storybook time at the end of your respite event. This increases the likelihood that the children are calm when the parents arrive, and allows the families to leave refreshed.

Encourage your volunteers to ask the parents how they spent their time away. The volunteers will be blessed as they compare the parents' tired faces at drop-off with their rested smiles at pick-up. It is a great idea for each buddy to try and have at least one positive story to share with the parent or caregiver as this can encourage them to come again.

If possible, it can be helpful to ask every family and every volunteer to complete an evaluation sheet after the event.☙

Parent evaluations can give you inspiring stories to use when you report to church leaders and recruit volunteers for the next event. This affirms the important work that your church is doing and how they are blessing families by providing much needed respite. If a parent has an issue, the evaluation can help your team make corrections and improve service in the future.

Volunteer evaluations assist in planning for future events. They can provide ideas of what worked and what did not. They might even suggest additional volunteers to contact for the next respite event. Include a question about whether or not they would be interested in serving on Sunday mornings, since respite volunteers are often excited to continue serving their new friends after spending time with them at the event.

It can be a rewarding and fruitful time to meet as a leadership team soon after the event to debrief, collect stories, and plan for how best to share those stories as you begin recruiting for your next event.

Fresh Water

For families affected by disability the opportunity for respite is a blessing of tremendous proportion. As these weary families walk through the daily difficulties of life with a disability, you and I have the privileged honor of digging wells and offering them a cup of fresh water—water that is refreshing, inviting and rare. The opportunity to model the gospel through a respite event is exciting, fun and with the right planning, incredibly effective. We pray that this book will, indeed, help you create a respite event so successful that you will want to repeat it many times. Bless you as you seek God's leading!

The *Irresistible* Church

Luke 14 commands Christ followers to "Go quickly . . . find the blind, the lame, and the crippled . . . and compel them to come in!" While this sounds inspiring and daunting, exciting and overwhelming, motivating and frightening, all at the same time, what does it actually mean? How do we live and function within the church in such a way that families affected by disability are compelled to walk through our doors to experience the body of Christ?

We can certainly *compel* them by offering programs, ministries, events, and other church activities, but what if the compelling aspect was more about heart, culture, acceptance and embracing? What if our churches were overflowing with the hope of Jesus Christ . . . a hope not simply for those who look the part or "fit in," but rather a hope to all, including the marginalized, the downtrodden and outcast?

Becoming *irresistible* is more than programs and activities—it is about a transformational work in our hearts . . . first as individuals and then as the body of Christ. *Irresistible* allows us to see each individual as he or she truly is: created in the image of God (Genesis 1:26-27), designed purposely as a masterpiece (Psalm 139:13-14), instilled with purpose, plans and dreams (Jeremiah 29:11), and a truly indispensable member of the kingdom of God (1 Corinthians 12:22).

Irresistible is a mindset, a perspective, an aware-ness. It is the ability to see the world through the eyes of Christ and love people where they are, knowing that God has designed an amazing future and hope for every person on this earth. *Irresistible* captures the heart of the church as it should be—how else do we explain the rapid growth and intense attraction to the church in the book of Acts? People were lining up to join this movement of people in spite of the intense persecution and ridicule. The heart of God was em-bodied through the people of God by the Spirit of God . . . and that is simply *irresistible*!

The Irresistible Church Series is designed to help not only shape and transform the heart of the Church, but also to provide the practical steps and activities to put *flesh* around the *heart* of the Church. Thank you for responding to the call to become *irresistible* - it will not happen overnight, but it will happen. As with all good things, it requires patience and perseverance, de-termination and dedication, and ultimately an under-lying trust in the faithfulness of God. May God bless you on this journey and be assured that you are not alone—there are many on the path of *irresistible*.

For more information or to join the community, please visit www.irresistiblechurch.org.

and Friends
INTERNATIONAL DISABILITY CENTER

Joni and Friends was established in 1979 by Joni Eareckson Tada, who at 17 was injured in a diving accident, leaving her a quadriplegic. Since its inception, Joni and Friends has been dedicated to extending the love and message of Christ to people who are affected by disability whether it is the disabled person, a family member, or friend. Our objective is to meet the physical, emotional, and spiritual needs of this group of people in practical ways.

Joni and Friends is committed to recruiting, training, and motivating new generations of people with disabilities to become leaders in their churches and communities. Today, the Joni and Friends International Disability Center serves as the administrative hub for an array of programs which provide outreach to thousands of families affected by disability around the globe. These include two radio programs, an award-winning television series, the Wheels for the World international wheelchair distribution ministry, Family Retreats which provide respite for those with disabilities and their families, Field Services to provide church training along with educational and inspirational resources at a local level, and the Christian Institute on Disability to establish a firm biblical worldview on disability-related issues.

From local neighborhoods to the far reaches of the world, Joni and Friends is striving to demonstrate to people affected by disability, in tangible ways, that God has not abandoned them—he is with them—providing love, hope, and eternal salvation.

Available Now in the Irresistible Church Series

Start with Hello
Introducing Your Church to Special Needs Ministry

Families with special needs often share that they desire two things in their church: accessibility and acceptance. Accessibility to existing structures, programs and people is an imperative. Acceptance with a sense of belonging by the others who also participate in the structures, programs and fellowship of the church is equally necessary. In this simple book you'll learn the five steps to becoming an accessible and accepting church.

To receive first notice of upcoming resources, including respite, inclusive worship and support groups, please contact us at churchrelations@joniandfriends.org.

Coming Soon in the Irresistible Church Series

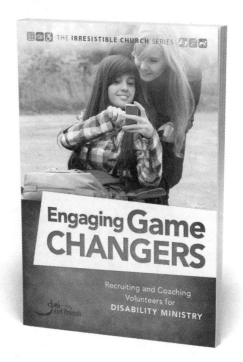

Engaging Game Changers
Recruiting and Coaching Volunteers for Disability Ministry

The breadth of impact any ministry has for the individuals they serve is dependent on the volunteers who are recruited to be the hands and feet of Jesus. This resource will train you as a ministry leader to identify and recruit, thoroughly train, then release volunteers who will serve families affected by special needs effectively and with the love of Christ.

To receive first notice of upcoming resources, including respite, inclusive worship and support groups, please contact us at churchrelations@joniandfriends.org.

Other Recommended Resources

Beyond Suffering®
Classic Edition

Beyond Suffering: A Christian View on Disability Ministry provides you with a roadmap to an effective and inspiring disability ministry. *Beyond Suffering* is a comprehensive course that gives an overview of the theological and practical underpinnings of the movement. It will equip you to think critically, compassionately and clearly about the complex issues that impact people with disabilities and their families and to confidently bring them the love of Christ.

ISBN: 978-0-9838484-0-0
272 pages · 8.5" x 11"
Includes CD-ROM

Beyond Suffering®
Student Edition

Beyond Suffering for the Next Generation: A Christian View on Disability Ministry will equip young people to consider the issues that affect people with disabilities and their families, and inspire them to action. Students who embrace this study will gain confidence to join a growing, worldwide movement that God is orchestrating to fulfill Luke 14:21-23: "Go out quickly into the streets and alleys of the town and bring in the poor, the crippled, the blind, and the lame.... so that my house will be full."

ISBN: 978-0-9838484-6-2
304 pages · 8.5" x 11"
Includes CD-ROM

Joni:
An Unforgettable Story

In this unforgettable autobiography, Joni reveals each step of her struggle to accept her disability and discover the meaning of her life. The hard-earned truths she discovers and the special ways God reveals his love are testimonies to faith's triumph over hardship and suffering. This new edition includes an afterword, in which Joni talks about the events that have occurred in her life since the book's original publication in 1976, including her marriage and the expansion of her worldwide ministry to families affected by disability.

ISBN: 978-0310240013
205 pages · Paperback

Customizable Resources from the Book

Available for Download at
http://www.joniandfriends.org/church-relations/

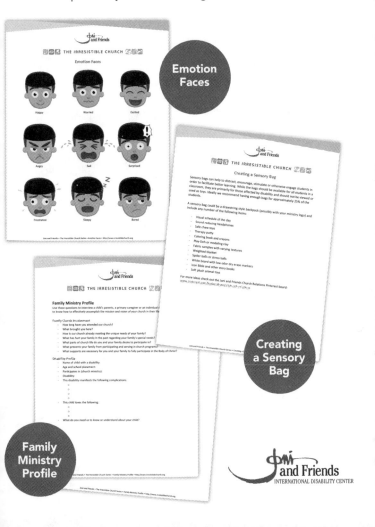

Emotion Faces

Creating a Sensory Bag

Family Ministry Profile